First Steps to

Office English

Tae Kudo

CENGAGE
Learning

First Steps to Office English [Text Only]

Tae Kudo

© 2011 Cengage Learning K.K.

ISBN: 978-4-86312-432-5

Cengage Learning K.K.
No 2 Funato Building 5th Floor
1-11-11 Kudankita, Chiyoda-ku
Tokyo 102-0073
Japan

Tel: 03-3511-4392
Fax: 03-3511-4391

まえがき

「実践的な英語力を身につけたい」「仕事で役に立つような英語を学びたい」という声をよく耳にします。大学へ入学し、多くの学生が、いわゆる「ビジネス英語」を学んでみたいという思いを多かれ少なかれ持つことだと思います。「ビジネス英語」関連のテキストは本屋の店頭にも多く見られますし、その需要は今後も一層高まっていくことでしょう。

本テキストは、「ビジネス英語」に関心を持つ学生のためのビジネス英語入門テキストです。「会社案内」「電話応対」などの日本国内で外国人と仕事で接する際に遭遇しそうな場面や、「ホテルのチェックイン」などの海外出張のときに役立つ場面を厳選しています。シンプルで簡潔な表現を中心としたコミュニケーションスキル養成のためのアクティビティが豊富に用意されていますので、英語に苦手意識を持っていても、スムーズに取り組むことができます。

また、スピーキングだけでなく、各ユニットのテーマに合ったライティング問題も設けています。リーディングとリスニングはTOEIC® TESTの問題形式に準じており、4技能すべてがバランスよく習得できるように作成しています。

本テキストの学習を通じて、「ビジネス英語」がより身近なものに感じられ、英語でのコミュニケーションに少しでも自信が持て、また楽しいものだと感じてもらえれば、著者としてこれ以上の幸せはありません。

末筆になりましたが、原稿執筆に際して貴重なアドバイスを下さった京都外国語大学の戸津井ペニー教授、本テキストの執筆のきっかけを与えて下さったセンゲージ ラーニングの小嶋里佳氏と原稿に大変丁寧なフィードバックを下さり、ご尽力頂いた吉田剛氏に心より感謝を申し上げます。最後に、いつも暖かく励ましサポートしてくれた家族に感謝の念を表したいと思います。

工藤多恵

Contents

■本テキストの構成と効果的な利用法

本テキストはスピーキング・アクティビティを中心に、リーディング、ライティング、リスニングの4技能すべてをカバーしたビジネス英語の入門テキストです。ビジネスでよく遭遇する場面をテーマに15ユニットで構成されています。各ユニットはすべて同じ構成で、それぞれのテーマにちなんだ様々なアクティビティが準備されています。また、教員用CDの収録音声を専用ウェブページでも利用できます。

以下では、ユニットの構成を具体的に述べ、各アクティビティの目的や最も効果的な利用法について説明します。

Key Expressions

ユニット内に出てくる重要表現を3つ選定して挙げています。学習後、テキストを見ずに言えるようになることが目標です。音声を聴いて発音を確認し、意味をしっかり理解しておきましょう。

Model Conversation

Key Expressions が実際に使われている会話をペアで練習します。まずは音声を聴いて本文を読み、内容を確認しましょう。読みづらい単語は音声を利用して練習し、慣れてきたら、本文を隠して音声を聴いてみるなどしてみましょう。

Cultural Tips

各ユニットのテーマに関連したトピックを取り上げて、日本とアメリカの「文化の違い」などを日本語と英語で簡単に説明しています。実際のコミュニケーションに役立つ内容です。

Class Work

Model Conversationよりも短いやり取りをテキストに頼らないで行えるようになることを狙いとしています。同じやり取りを色々な相手と繰り返し練習することによって、楽しみながら取り組み、発話に自信を持つことが期待されています。

Reading

各ユニットのテーマに沿ったTOEIC形式（Part 7）の演習問題です。質問文を先に読んでから、問題を解きましょう。わからない単語はすぐに辞書を引かず、文脈から意味を考えてみてください。それから辞書で確認すると頭に残りやすくなります。

Pair Work

Model Conversationを基にした会話練習です。自分で必要な情報に置き換えて相手に伝えましょう。また、会話から得られた内容をメモに取るため、相手の話をしっかり聴くことが大切です。ここでは役割になりきって話してみてください。

Writing

特にReadingの内容に沿った簡単なライティング課題です。ユニットによって、並び替えや空所補充など様々な形式がありますが、まずは何も見ずに取り組んでみましょう。

Listening

ユニットのまとめとしてTOEIC形式（Part 2, 3, 4）の演習問題に挑戦します。音声を何度も聴いて、正答を考えてみましょう。Part IIではPart Iよりも長い会話や英文が出題されます。まずは質問を読んで、ポイントを考えながら音声を聴いてください。わからない単語があっても、あまり意識し過ぎず、大意を把握することに努めましょう。

"It's nice to meet you."

Introduction

⚑ Goal

Introducing yourself and exchanging personal information

自己紹介の表現や初対面の際の簡単な受け答えの仕方を学びます

Key Expressions

··· ▼ 🎧 02

Listen and repeat the following expressions.

1. It's nice to meet you.
2. What do you do?
3. Please call me Naoko.

Model Conversation

··· ▼ 🎧 03

Practice the following dialogue with your partner.

A: Hello, I'm Naoko Yamada. It's nice to meet you. ┈► I'm pleased

B: Nice to meet you, Ms. Yamada.

A: Oh, please call me Naoko.

B: OK, Naoko. I'm Ken Adams. Please call me Ken. ┈► All right

(shake hands)

A: What do you do, Ken?

B: I work for ABC Computing in New York. I am an engineer. How about you, Naoko? ┈► a sales representative

A: I do office work. I'm an office assistant. I work in Osaka.

B: Oh, I see.

Class Work

· ▼

Move around the class and practice the conversation. Write down the names of the people you meet in the chart. Don't forget to shake hands and make eye contact.

Hi, I'm _____.
    your name
    It's nice to meet you.

Nice to meet you, too.

I'm _Naoko Yamada_.
    your partner's name

Ex.	Naoko Yamada	

☀ Cultural Tips

In English-speaking countries, it is important to shake hands when you meet someone for the first time. It should be firm and you should maintain eye contact. Exchanging business cards or how you give and/or receive a card is not as important as shaking hands. You can give your card, perhaps, after shaking hands.

英語圏の人に自己紹介をする際、大切なのは堅い握手です。手の平をしっかり合わせて、相手の目を見ながら堅い握手を交わしましょう。日本と異なり、名刺の交換や渡し方はあまり重要ではありません。握手の後で渡せばよいでしょう。

Reading

Read the following business cards and select the best answer to each question.

XYZ Printing, Inc.

Gina Rossi
Secretary

15 London St. London, W2 1HL UK
Tel: (020) 8803-5225 Ext. 225
E-mail: rossi@xyz.co.uk

Ken Adams
System Engineer

ABC
COMPUTING

325 Central Avenue
New York, NY 10010 USA
Tel: (212) 204-9811
E-mail: ka@abc.com

 Southeast Airlines

Julie Yang
Customer Service Representative

Changi Airport
Singapore 918146
(65) 6599-6886
julie@southeast.co.sg

Wahoo Corporation **Wahoo**

Toshi Yoshioka
Marketing Manager

6-5 Umeda, Kita-ku, Osaka-shi
Osaka 530-0001 Japan
Tel: (06) 8798-0200
Fax: (06) 8798-0100
tyoshioka@wahoo.co.jp

1. What does Ms. Rossi do?
  (A) She exchanges business cards.
  (B) She is a photographer.
  (C) She works for XYZ Printing, Inc.

2. What is Mr. Yoshioka's fax number?
  (A) (06) 8798-0200   (B) (020) 8803-5225   (C) (06) 8798-0100

3. Which company does Mr. Adams work for?
  (A) XYZ Printing, Inc.   (B) ABC Computing   (C) Southeast Airlines

4. What is Ms. Yang's e-mail address?
  (A) julie@southeast.co.sg   (B) ka@abc.com   (C) rossi@xyz.co.uk

Pair Work

Student A

Part I

1. Look at the business card of Gina Rossi in **Reading** (p. 10). Instead of her name, use your own name. The other information on the card is yours. Now, using the pattern in **Model Conversation** (p. 8), introduce yourself to your partner. You start the conversation.

2. You are the same person, but your partner starts the conversation this time. Write down his/her information in the chart below.

Part II

1. Look at the business card of Ken Adams in **Reading** (p. 10). Instead of his name, use your own name. The other information on the card is yours. Now, using the pattern in **Model Conversation** (p. 8), introduce yourself to your partner. Your partner starts the conversation.

2. You are the same person, but you start the conversation this time. Write down his/her information in the chart below.

Part III
Change partners and repeat the tasks above.

Full name	Nickname	Job	Working place
Ex. Ken Adams	Ken	engineer	New York

Student B

Part I

1. Look at the business card of Julie Yang in **Reading** (p. 10). Instead of her name, use your own name. The other information on the card is yours. Now, using the pattern in **Model Conversation** (p. 8), introduce yourself to your partner. Your partner starts the conversation.

2. You are the same person, but you start the conversation this time. Write down his/her information in the chart below.

Part II

1. Look at the business card of Toshi Yoshioka in **Reading** (p. 10). Instead of his name, use your own name. The other information on the card is yours. Now, using the pattern in **Model Conversation** (p. 8), introduce yourself to your partner. You start the conversation.

2. You are the same person, but your partner starts the conversation this time. Write down his/her information in the chart below.

Part III
Change partners and repeat the tasks above.

Full name	Nickname	Job	Working place
Ex. Naoko Yamada	Naoko	office assistant	Osaka

Writing

●● ▼

Make your own business card.

Listening

●● ▼

Part I: Question and Response

Listen to the CD. You will hear a question or statement followed by three
responses. Select the best response to the question or statement.

 04 05

1. (A) (B) (C)   **2.** (A) (B) (C)

Part II: Short Conversation

Listen to the CD. You will hear a short conversation.
Select the best answer to each question.

 06

1. What does Naoko do?

  (A) She works at Tokyo Disneyland.

  (B) She works in Japan.

  (C) She is an assistant.

2. Where is this conversation most likely to take place?

  (A) In a supermarket.

  (B) In an amusement park.

  (C) In an office.

"What does 'FYI' mean?"

Clarifying Meanings

Goal

Asking a word's meaning and to repeat or slow down

ゆっくり言ってもらうように頼む表現や、わからない言葉の意味を尋ねたり、聞き直したりする方法を学びます

Key Expressions

▼ 07

Listen and repeat the following expressions.

1. What does "FYI" mean?
2. How do you say *keitai* in English?
3. Sorry? Could you say that again?

Model Conversation

▼ 08 09

Practice the following dialogues with your partner.

1. **A:** May I ask you something?   → Can
   B: Sure.
   A: What does "FYI" mean?   → stand for
   B: It means "for your information."
   A: I didn't know that. Thank you.
   B: You're welcome.   → No problem.

2. **A:** How do you say *keitai* in English?
   B: Cell phone.
   A: Sorry? Could you say that again?   → speak more slowly
   B: Cell phone.
   A: Oh, OK. Thanks.
   B: No problem.   → You're welcome.

Class Work

Choose one word from the left box to make a question. Respond to the question by using the word from the right box. Move around the class and practice the conversation. Write down the information in the chart.

keitai [携帯電話]	*mensetsu* [面接]	boss	meeting
arubaito [アルバイト]	*joshi* [上司]	extension	customer
kokyaku [顧客]	*naisen* [内線]	business card	part-time job
busho [部署]	*kaigi* [会議]	interview	department
meishi [名刺]	*rirekisho* [履歴書]	clerk	cell phone
jimuin [事務員]		resume	

How do you say _keitai_ in English?
word in Japanese

Thank you.

Cell phone .
word in English

No problem.

Partner's name	Word in Japanese	Word in English
Ex. Miki Kishimoto	keitai	cell phone

Reading

Read the following advertisement and select the best answer to each question.

FINDAJOB.COM

Bilingual Server Wanted. New American Restaurant is currently interviewing for server positions. We are looking for someone w/ the following: lang. skills (English and Japanese), ability to work under pressure, and positive attitude. Must be able to work on weekends. Send resume to Personnel Dept., 9-8-12 Shinsaibashi, Chuo-ku, Osaka-shi, Osaka 542-0085 immed.

FYI: http://www.nar.com

---

1. What position is being advertised?

  (A) Bilingual teacher   (B) Waiter/Waitress   (C) Language partner

2. What does "immed." mean?

  (A) As soon as possible   (B) Currently   (C) Without hurrying

3. Which of the following is most likely to be important for this position?

  (A) Feeling a lot of pressure   (B) Speaking two languages

  (C) Working on weekdays

4. What should you do if you are interested in this position?

  (A) Send your resume   (B) Check their website   (C) Call the manager

---

Cultural Tips

Have you pretended that you understood what someone said, but you didn't? If you do not understand, ask them to repeat or slow down or tell them you do not understand. The person who is speaking will appreciate your honesty. Instead of using facial expressions, just ask, "Could you say that again?" "Could you speak more slowly?" or "What does XXX mean?"

相手が何を言っているのかはっきりわからないときでも、わかっているふりをすることが結構多くありませんか。相手の言っていることがわからない場合は、「もう一度言ってもらえますか?」「ゆっくり話してもらえますか?」「×××はどういう意味ですか?」などと必ず尋ねるようにしましょう。それでも意味がわからないときは、正直に「すみませんが、意味がわかりません」と言う方が好ましいでしょう。どのような場合も表情で訴えかけるのではなく、言葉ではっきりと質問し、コミュニケーションを図ることが大切です。

Pair Work

....

Student A

Part I

Look at the chart below. Some definitions are missing. Ask your partner by using the pattern in **Model Conversation 1** (p. 14) and fill in the blanks. You make a question first. Then, take turns with your partner.

Abbreviation	Definition (Meaning)
Ex. FYI	for your information
mtg.	
appt.	appointment
co.	
ASAP	as soon as possible
St.	
Rd.	road
mo.	
min.	minute

Part II

Look at the chart below. Some English words are missing. Ask your partner by using the pattern in **Model Conversation 2** (p. 14) and fill in the blanks. Your partner makes a question first. Then, take turns.

Word in Japanese	Word in English
Ex. keitai [携帯電話]	cell phone
uketsuke [受付]	receptionist
doryo [同僚]	
dengon [伝言]	message
hisho [秘書]	

Student B

Part I

Look at the chart. Some definitions are missing. Ask your partner by using the pattern in **Model Conversation 1** (p. 14) and fill in the blanks. Your partner makes a question first. Then, take turns.

Abbreviation	Definition (Meaning)
Ex. FYI	for your information
mtg.	meeting
appt.	
co.	company
ASAP	
St.	street
Rd.	
mo.	month
min.	

Part II

Look at the chart. Some English words are missing. Ask your partner by using the pattern in **Model Conversation 2** (p. 14) and fill in the blanks. You make a question first. Then, take turns with your partner.

Word in Japanese	Word in English
Ex. keitai [携帯電話]	cell phone
uketsuke [受付]	
doryo [同僚]	colleague
dengon [伝言]	
hisho [秘書]	secretary

Writing

Part I

Miki Kishimoto wrote the following letter to the manager of New American Restaurant in **Reading** (p. 16). Put the letter in the right order.

☐ → ☐ → ☐ → ☐ → ☐ → ☐ → ☐ → ☐ → ☐ → ☐

(A) I am currently a junior at Shin-Nihon University and majoring in English. I have some experience in working as a server at Moonbucks for the past two years.

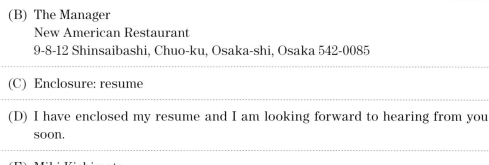

(B) The Manager
New American Restaurant
9-8-12 Shinsaibashi, Chuo-ku, Osaka-shi, Osaka 542-0085

(C) Enclosure: resume

(D) I have enclosed my resume and I am looking forward to hearing from you soon.

(E) Miki Kishimoto

(F) Dear Manager,

(G) *Miki Kishimoto*

(H) April 27, 2012

(I) I am interested in the position of Bilingual Server, which was posted on FINDAJOB.COM.

(J) Sincerely,

Part II
Write your mailing address in English.

Listening

Part I: Question and Response

Listen to the CD. You will hear a question or statement followed by three responses. Select the best response to the question or statement.

1. (A) (B) (C)   **2.** (A) (B) (C)

Part II: Short Talk

Listen to the CD. You will hear a short talk.
Select the best answer to each question.

1. What is the speaker talking about?

(A) The French dish   (B) The French phrase   (C) The French party

2. What does "RSVP" mean?

(A) "Please respond."   (B) "Please attend the party."   (C) "Please invite me."

"May I speak to Mr. Yoshioka?"

Phone Conversation [1]

⚑ Goal

Answering the phone and transferring the call

電話の応対と取り次ぎの方法を学びます

Key Expressions

Listen and repeat the following expressions. 13

1. May I speak to Mr. Yoshioka?
2. This is Naoko Yamada speaking.
3. This is Tom Hoffman from Sunlight Company.

Model Conversation

Practice the following dialogues with your partner. 14 15

1. **A:** Hello, Wahoo Corporation. This is Naoko Yamada speaking.
   B: May I speak to Ms. Heather Rowan? ► Could
   A: Uh, no, I think you have the wrong number.
   B: Oh, sorry.

2. **A:** Hello, Wahoo Corporation. This is Naoko Yamada speaking.
   B: This is Tom Hoffman from Sunlight Company.
   A: Sorry? Could you say your name again? ► Pardon?
   B: Tom Hoffman.
   A: Oh, hi, Mr. Hoffman. May I help you?
   B: May I speak to Mr. Yoshioka? ► Could
   A: Please hold. I'll put you through to Mr. Yoshioka. ► Just a moment.
   B: Thank you.

Class Work

· ▼

First, ask your partner if you can speak to another classmate. Next, ask to speak to someone who is NOT in your class. Move around the class and practice the conversation. Stand back-to-back and write down the information in the chart.

May I speak to _Ms. Tina Collins_ ?
your classmate's name

Please hold.
I'll put you through to _Tina Collins_ .
your classmate's name

May I speak to _Mr. Hiroki Sato_ ?
unknown name

You have the wrong number.

	Partner's name	Classmate's name	Unknown name
Ex.	Naoko Yamada	Tina Collins	Hiroki Sato

☀ Cultural Tips

When you answer the phone and hear English, do you panic? Regardless of the language, you should ask for 1) his/her name, 2) whom he/she would like to speak to, and 3) if that person is not available, ask for contact information. If you do not understand, ask again. It is important to always double check and confirm what you heard.

電話を受け、突然英語が聞こえてきたら焦ってしまうことがあるかもしれません。電話の応対では、1) 名前を尋ねる、2) 電話を取り次ぐ、3) 取り次げない場合、相手の連絡先や希望を聞くことができればよいでしょう。わからない場合は必ず聞き返して内容を確認し、間違いのないように落ち着いて対応しましょう。

Reading

Read the following list and select the best answer to each question.

Customer Phone Number List

	Company	Name (Last name, First name)		Phone	Extension
1.	ABC Computing	Johnson, Sara	(Ms.)	(212) 204-9811	
2.	China Corporation	Lee, Chang	(Mr.)	(03) 3274-6921	
3.	Happy Int'l Travel	Oliveira, Carlos	(Mr.)	(212) 151-2255	267
4.	Bay Shore Hotel	Smith, Mandy	(Ms.)	(603) 715-8800	802
5.	Southeast Airlines	Gomez, Elena	(Ms.)	(65) 6599-6886	
6.	Sunlight Co., Ltd.	Hoffman, Tom	(Mr.)	(06) 6318-9645	512
7.	Western Food Service	Davis, Tim	(Mr.)	(415) 528-2166	221
8.	XYZ Printing, Inc.	Rossi, Gina	(Ms.)	(020) 8803-5225	225

1. What is Mr. Oliveira's phone number?
   (A) (212) 151-2255   (B) 267   (C) (212) 2255-267

2. How many phone numbers are there on the list?
   (A) 8   (B) 12   (C) 13

3. What is the area code in Ms. Rossi's phone number?
   (A) 020   (B) 8803   (C) 225

4. How do you say Ms. Smith's phone number?
   (A) Six-oh-three, seven-one-five, eight-double-oh-double
   (B) Six-oh-three, seven-one-five, double-eight-double-oh
   (C) Six-oh-three, seven-one-five, eight-oh-doubles

Pair Work

•• ▼

Student A

Part I

1. You are a secretary at Wahoo Corporation. Using the pattern in **Model Conversation 2** (p. 20), answer the phone and write down the caller's information in the chart below. Sit back-to-back.

2. You are one of the people on the list in **Reading** (p. 22). Using the pattern in **Model Conversation 2** (p. 20), call Wahoo Corporation and ask for Mr. Yoshioka. Sit back-to-back.

Part II
Change partners and repeat the tasks above.

First name	Last name	Company
Ex. Tom	Hoffman	Sunlight Company

Student B

Part I

1. You are one of the people on the list in **Reading** (p. 22). Using the pattern in **Model Conversation 2** (p. 20), call Wahoo Corporation and ask for Mr. Yoshioka. Sit back-to-back.

2. You are a secretary at Wahoo Corporation. Using the pattern in **Model Conversation 2** (p. 20), answer the phone and write down the caller's information in the chart below. Sit back-to-back.

Part II

Change partners and repeat the tasks above.

First name	Last name	Company
Ex. Tom	Hoffman	Sunlight Company

Writing

· ▾ 16

Listen to the CD and fill in the blanks with appropriate phone numbers.

Phone Numbers

Mr. Eric Tucker:

Ms. Lisa Brown:

Dr. Powell:

Joe's Seafood House:

Phone Company:

Listening

· ▾

Part I: Question and Response

Listen to the CD. You will hear a question or statement followed by three responses. Select the best response to the question or statement.

17
18

1. (A) (B) (C)   **2.** (A) (B) (C)

Part II: Short Conversation

Listen to the CD. You will hear a short conversation. Select the best answer to each question.

 19

1. What's XYZ Printing's phone number?

(A) 8803-5525   (B) 8803-5225   (C) 8803-5252

2. Why was the man sorry?

(A) Because he borrowed the phone.

(B) Because he made a mistake.

(C) Because he spoke on the phone.

"May I take a message?"

Phone Conversation [2]

Goal

Answering the phone and taking a message

前のユニットに続き、電話の応対方法と、
伝言の書き方を学びます

Key Expressions

Listen and repeat the following expressions.

1. May I take a message?
2. How do you spell your name?
3. May I have your name?

Model Conversation

Practice the following dialogue with your partner.

A: Hello, Wahoo Corporation. This is Naoko Yamada speaking.

B: This is Chang Lee from China Corporation. Could I speak to Mr. Yoshioka?

A: I'm sorry. He is not available right now.   ➤ He is in a meeting
May I take a message?   ➤ Would you like to leave

B: Yes. Could you ask him to call me back?

A: Sure. May I have your name again?

B: It's Chang Lee.

A: How do you spell your name?

B: Chang, C-H-A-N-G, Lee, L-E-E.

A: L as in London?

B: Yes.

A: And may I have your phone number?

B: Sure. It's area code (03) 3274-6921.

A: I'll pass along your message. Thank you for calling.   ➤ give him

Class Work

• ▼

Ask your partner's name and phone number. Move around the class and practice the conversation. Stand back-to-back and write down the information in the chart.

May I have your name?

It's _Naoko Yamada_ .
your partner's name

May I have your phone number?

It's _080-2189-0851_ .
your partner's number

Partner's name	Partner's phone number
Ex. Naoko Yamada	080-2189-0851

-ᵜ- Cultural Tips

In North America, you might see some phone numbers which include both numbers and letters or words, like 1 (800) BEST CAR. 1 (800) is toll-free and BEST CAR is 237-8227. By using the name of the company, store or a specific item, people are most likely to remember the number.

北米では、広告や宣伝で 1 (800) BEST CAR のような数字と短いフレーズを組み合わせたものをよく見かけます。1 (800) はフリーダイヤル、BEST CAR は実は 237-8227 で、電話番号なのです。このように会社や店、商品の名前などを用いることで、人々の記憶に残りやすく、注意をひく効果をねらっています。

Reading

Read the following form and select the best answer to each question.

Telephone Message

For: Scott

Date: 5/9/12

Time: 11:20 a.m.

(Mr.)Ms.: Davis

of Western Food Service   called

Phone #: (415)   528-2166   ×221
           area code   extension

Message: He wants to talk to you about a presentation for a new product. He'll call you back tomorrow morning.

Taken by: Naoko

1. Who called?

(A) Scott   (B) Mr. Davis   (C) Naoko

2. What time did the person call?

(A) At 5:09   (B) At 11:20   (C) At 2:21

3. Why did the person call?

(A) To discuss the new product

(B) To talk to Naoko

(C) To go out with Scott

4. What will the person do tomorrow?

(A) Give a presentation

(B) Call again

(C) Sell a new product

Pair Work

••

Student A

Part I

You are a secretary at Wahoo Corporation. Using the pattern in **Model Conversation** (p. 26), answer the phone and complete the message form. Sit back-to-back. You will receive two phone calls.

Telephone Message		Telephone Message	
For:	_____	For:	_____
Date:	_____	Date:	_____
Time:	_____	Time:	_____
Mr/Ms:	_____	Mr/Ms:	_____
of _____ called		of _____ called	
Phone #:	_____	Phone #:	_____
area code extension		area code extension	
☐ Please call back		☐ Please call back	
☐ Will call back		☐ Will call back	
Taken by:	_____	Taken by:	_____

Part II

Using the pattern in **Model Conversation** (p. 26), call Wahoo Corporation twice. Sit back-to-back. You are Gina Rossi for the first phone call, and then Carlos Oliveira for the next. Follow the instructions below.

1. You are Gina Rossi from XYZ Printing, Inc. You want to talk to Mr. Yoshioka. Ask his secretary to call you back at (020) 8803-5225.

2. You are Carlos Oliveira from Happy International Travel. You want to talk to Ms. Collins. Ask her secretary to call you back at (212) 151-2255.

Part I

Using the pattern in **Model Conversation** (p. 26), call Wahoo Corporation twice. Sit back-to-back. You are Elena Gomez for the first phone call, and then Tim Davis for the next. Follow the instructions below.

1. You are Elena Gomez from Southeast Airlines. You want to talk to Mr. Robinson. Ask his secretary to call you back at (65) 6599-6886.

2. You are Tim Davis from Western Food Service. You want to talk to Ms. Yamada. Ask her secretary to call you back at (415) 528-2166.

Part II

You are a secretary at Wahoo Corporation. Using the pattern in **Model Conversation** (p. 26), answer the phone and complete the message form. Sit back-to-back. You will receive two phone calls.

Telephone Message

For: _____

Date: _____

Time: _____

Mr/Ms: _____

of _____ called

Phone #: _____

area code   extension

☐ Please call back

☐ Will call back

Taken by: _____

Telephone Message

For: _____

Date: _____

Time: _____

Mr/Ms: _____

of _____ called

Phone #: _____

area code   extension

☐ Please call back

☐ Will call back

Taken by: _____

Writing

• ○

Listen to the CD and complete the form.

While You Were Out

To: _____

Date: _____   Time: _____

Mr/Ms: _____ of _____ called

Phone #: _____
          area code   extension

Message: _____

_____

Taken by: _____

Listening

• ○

Part I: Question and Response

Listen to the CD. You will hear a question or statement followed by three responses. Select the best response to the question or statement.

1. (A) (B) (C)   **2.** (A) (B) (C)

Part II: Short Talk

Listen to the CD. You will hear a short talk.
Select the best answer to each question.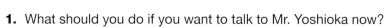

1. What should you do if you want to talk to Mr. Yoshioka now?

(A) Wait for his call   (B) Call his assistant   (C) Visit him

2. How long will Mr. Yoshioka be away?

(A) From May 29 to June 6

(B) From May 29 to June 16

(C) From May 19 to June 16

"I have a headache."

Calling in Sick

Goal

Asking how someone is and talking about health problems

体調が優れないときや病欠の際に使う表現を学びます

Key Expressions

26

Listen and repeat the following expressions.

1. What's wrong?
2. I have a headache.
3. I hope you feel better soon.

Model Conversation

27

Practice the following dialogue with your partner.

A: Hello, Wahoo Corporation. This is Scott Robinson speaking.

B: This is Naoko.

A: Hi, Naoko, how are you?

B: Well, actually, I'm not feeling very well.

A: What's wrong?

B: I have a very bad headache.

A: Oh, that's too bad. Toshi called in sick, too.   ⊦► I'm sorry to hear that

B: It seems everyone is sick now.

A: I hope you feel better soon.   ⊦► Take care.

B: Thanks.

Class Work

• ▼

Choose one problem from the box for your response. Move around the class and practice the conversation. Write down the information in the chart.

What's wrong?

I have a _headache_.

That's too bad.

headache
cold
stomachache
toothache
fever
hangover

Partner's name	Partner's problem
Ex. Toshi Yoshioka	headache

🔆 Cultural Tips

How would you answer the question "How are you?"? You may answer "I'm fine, thank you." or you may say "So so." In English, "So so." is not very common. "OK." and "All right." are more like "So so." in Japanese. "Good." or "Fine." are good answers if you are not sick. "Bad." is used when you are very sick.

"How are you?" と聞かれると、"I'm fine, thank you." と答える人もいれば、日本語でよく使う「まあまあ」という意味で "So so." と答える人もいるかもしれません。しかし実際は、このような場合に "So so." はほとんど使われず、日本の感覚の「まあまあ」は、英語では "OK." または "All right." くらいに当たるでしょう。英語圏では、文化的に前向きに答える場合が多いため、"Good." や "Fine." と答えるのが一般的です。"Bad." は本当に体調が悪いときに使う表現のため、むやみに連発しないようにしましょう。

Reading

. . . . ▼

Read the following e-mail and select the best answer to each question.

Sent: July 12, 11:05 a.m.
From: nyamada@wahoo.co.jp
To: srobinson@wahoo.co.jp
Cc: tyoshioka@wahoo.co.jp
Subject: sick leave

Dear Mr. Robinson,

As I said on the phone this morning, I'm not feeling well.
Actually I've got the flu. My doctor says I need to take about
a week off.

I'll let you know exactly when I can go back to work.

Thank you for your understanding.

Sincerely,
Naoko Yamada

---

1. Why did Ms. Yamada send this e-mail?
   (A) To talk to the doctor   (B) To ask for sick leave   (C) To go back to work

2. When is Ms. Yamada most likely to go back to work?
   (A) On July 12   (B) On July 14   (C) On July 19

3. Who received this e-mail?
   (A) Mr. Robinson   (B) Mr. Yoshioka   (C) Mr. Robinson and Mr. Yoshioka

4. Which of the following is TRUE?
   (A) Ms. Yamada has the flu.
   (B) Ms. Yamada didn't go to see a doctor.
   (C) Ms. Yamada knows what date she can go back to work.

Pair Work

Student A

Part I

You are a secretary at Wahoo Corporation. Using the pattern in **Model Conversation** (p. 32), answer the phone and write down the caller's information in the chart below. Sit back-to-back. You will receive four phone calls.

Caller	Health problem	Another sick person
Beth		the manager
Mike		Lisa
Jenny		the assistant
Roy		Jack

Part II

1. You are Tina. You don't feel well today. Using the pattern in **Model Conversation** (p. 32), call your company and tell the secretary about your health problem. Write down the name of another sick person in the chart. Sit back-to-back. Your partner starts the conversation.

2. After the first phone call as Tina, you will role play other people on the list and make three more phone calls.

Your name	Health problem	Another sick person
Tina	stomachache	
Ben	fever	
Mary	cold	
Sam	headache	

Part I

1. You are Beth. You don't feel well today. Using the pattern in **Model Conversation** (p. 32), call your company and tell the secretary about your health problem. Write down the name of another sick person in the chart. Sit back-to-back. Your partner starts the conversation.

2. After the first phone call as Beth, you will role play other people on the list and make three more phone calls.

Your name	Health problem	Another sick person
Beth	very bad headache	
Mike	toothache	
Jenny	fever	
Roy	cold	

Part II

You are a secretary at Wahoo Corporation. Using the pattern in **Model Conversation** (p. 32), answer the phone and write down the caller's information in the chart below. Sit back-to-back. You will receive four phone calls.

Caller	Health problem	Another sick person
Tina		Tony
Ben		the boss
Mary		Eric
Sam		the secretary

Writing

• ▼

You have a very bad cold. Your doctor suggests that you should take
a few days off. Complete the following e-mail message to your boss.

Dear Mr. Robinson,

(   ) (   ) a very bad cold. (   )
(   ) (   ) I need to (   ) a few
days (   ).

I'll (   ) (   ) (   ) exactly when
I can go back to work.

Thank you for your (   ).

Regards,
(   ) (   )
your first name   *your last name*

Listening

• ▼

Part I: Question and Response

Listen to the CD. You will hear a question or statement followed by three
responses. Select the best response to the question or statement.

1. (A) (B) (C)   **2.** (A) (B) (C)

Part II: Short Conversation

Listen to the CD. You will hear a short conversation.
Select the best answer to each question.

1. Where is Tina most likely to be now?

(A) At the company   (B) At home   (C) At a restaurant

2. What's wrong with Tina?

(A) She has the wrong number.

(B) She is away for a week.

(C) She is very sick.

Goal

Talking about schedules and rescheduling appointments

予定を調整したり、変更したりする
方法を学びます

Key Expressions

31

Listen and repeat the following expressions.

1. You have an appointment with Mr. Yoshioka at 2:00.
2. I have another appointment at 9:30.
3. Can you change the meeting from 9:00 to 10:30?

Model Conversation

32

Practice the following dialogue with your partner.

A: Do you know my schedule for Monday? ► tomorrow

B: There will be a meeting with the sales ► conference call
manager at 9:00. Then you have an
appointment with your dentist at 1:00. You
need to leave the office around 12:45.

A: Hmm…, actually, I have another
appointment at 9:30. Can you change the
meeting from 9:00 to 10:30? ► conference call

B: I will call the person in charge to make the ► contact
change.

A: Thank you.

おはよう

Class Work

Ask your partner what time he/she usually leaves for school or work. Respond to the question by using your real information. Move around the class and practice the conversation. Write down the information in the chart.

What time do you usually leave for school?

Usually around 7:30 a.m.

Partner's name	Leaving for...	Time
Ex. Miki Kishimoto	school / work	7:30 a.m.
	school / work	
	school / work	
	school / work	
	school / work	
	school / work	
	school / work	
	school / work	

Cultural Tips

Do you know the stereotype that American people are not strict about time, while Japanese people are very strict? If you are meeting American friends, it is not a problem if you are a little late. However, it is important to be on time for business in both countries. If you think you will be late, call the person immediately to let him or her know your arrival time.

「日本人は時間厳守で、アメリカ人は時間にルーズ」というようなイメージはありませんか。友だち同士の約束であったり、家に招待されたりというようなときであれば、多少時間に遅れても大して問題はないでしょう。しかし、ビジネスではどちらの国も時間厳守であることに注意しておきましょう。また遅刻することがわかったらすぐに連絡し、大体の到着予定を相手に知らせるマナーも忘れずに。

Reading

Read the following schedule and select the best answer to each question.

Ken's Schedule

9:00–10:30	mtg. w/ sales manager
1:00–2:00	appointment w/ dentist
3:00–	conference call
6:00–	appointment with Toshi @ Joe's Seafood House

1. What time will Ken go to see a doctor?

(A) At 9:00 a.m.

(B) At 1:00 p.m

(C) At 3:00 p.m.

2. Who will Ken meet at 9:00?

(A) His dentist

(B) Mr. Call

(C) The sales manager

3. Where is Ken's appointment with Toshi?

(A) In Ken's house

(B) In Toshi's office

(C) In a restaurant

4. What time will the conference call be held?

(A) At 1:00 p.m.

(B) At 3:00 p.m.

(C) At 6:00 p.m.

Pair Work

• •

Student A

Part I

1. You work for Wahoo Corporation. Using the pattern in **Model Conversation** (p. 38), ask your secretary about your schedule for Tuesday. Write down the new schedule in the chart.

2. Now, ask about your schedule for Wednesday. Write down the new schedule in the chart.

MAY 12, TUESDAY	MAY 13, WEDNESDAY
11:30–12:00 appointment	2:00–2:30 appointment

Part II

You are a secretary at Wahoo Corporation. Your boss will ask you about his/her schedule. Using the pattern in **Model Conversation** (p. 38), talk to him/her.

MAY 21, THURSDAY	MAY 22, FRIDAY
9:00–10:30 discussion with CEO 11:00–12:00 plant tour	2:00–3:00 mtg. w/ marketing manager 6:00– doctor appointment (need to leave office 10 minutes early; 5:50)

Part I

You are a secretary at Wahoo Corporation. Your boss will ask you about his/her schedule. Using the pattern in **Model Conversation** (p. 38), talk to him/her.

MAY 12, TUESDAY	MAY 13, WEDNESDAY
9:00–11:00 meeting w/ staff members 11:30–12:30 conference call	2:15–4:30 presentation at sales dept. 6:00– dinner at Big Steak House (need to leave office 15 minutes early; 5:45)

Part II

1. You work for Wahoo Corporation. Using the pattern in **Model Conversation** (p. 38), ask your secretary about your schedule for Thursday. Write down the new schedule in the chart.

2. Now, ask about your schedule for Friday. Write down the new schedule in the chart.

MAY 21, THURSDAY	MAY 22, FRIDAY
10:45–11:15 appointment	2:00–2:30 appointment

Writing

Write your own schedule for a typical non-school or non-work day.

DATE:

9:00–

11:00–

12:00–

1:00–

3:00–

5:00–

7:00–

9:00–

Listening

Part I: Question and Response

Listen to the CD. You will hear a question or statement followed by three responses. Select the best response to the question or statement.

33
34

1. (A) (B) (C)　　**2.** (A) (B) (C)

Part II: Short Talk

Listen to the CD. You will hear a short talk.
Select the best answer to each question.

35

1. What is the speaker talking about?

(A) The schedule for the meeting

(B) Discussion about topics for the meeting

(C) Participants in the meeting

2. What time will Mr. Yoshioka give a presentation?

(A) At 9:30　　(B) At 9:45　　(C) At 10:15

"Would you like something to drink?"

Making Offers

Goal

Offering something and telling about preferences

訪問者を案内したり、飲み物などを
提供したりする際の表現を学びます

Key Expressions

Listen and repeat the following expressions. 36

1. Would you like something to drink?
2. How would you like your coffee?
3. Here you are.

Model Conversation

Practice the following dialogue with your partner. 37

A: Hello. I'm Ken Adams from ABC Computing.
   I have an appointment with Mr. Yoshioka at 2:30.

B: Hello, Mr. Adams. Come this way, please. *(pause)*
   Please have a seat.

A: Thank you.

B: Would you like something to drink? We have   ⊢► care for
   coffee, tea, and juice.

A: Tea, please.

B: How would you like your tea?

A: I'd like it straight, please.   ⊢► With milk

B: No problem. *(pause)* Here you are.

A: Thank you.

Class Work

Ask your partner how he/she wants to drink coffee or tea. Respond to the question by using the phrase from the box. Move around the class and practice the conversation. Write down the information in the chart.

How would you like your _coffee_ ?

With sugar and milk , please.

Here you are.

Thank you.

With sugar and milk
With sugar and cream
With sugar and lemon
With sugar
With milk
With cream
With lemon
I'd like it black
I'd like it straight

Partner's name	Drink	What he/she wants
Ex. Naoko Yamada	(coffee)/ tea	with sugar and milk
	coffee / tea	
	coffee / tea	
	coffee / tea	
	coffee / tea	
	coffee / tea	
	coffee / tea	
	coffee / tea	

☀ Cultural Tips

In Japan, when you are offered something, you may bow or say "Domo." or "Sumimasen." to express your gratitude. In English, "I'm sorry." is used to express an apology. Saying "Thank you." is most common. Say "Thank you." with a smile. Also, say "Thank you." for a minor thing like someone holding the door open for you.

日本では、何かしてもらったときには、軽く頭を下げたり、「どうも」「すみません」という表現を使ったりして謝意を表すことがあります。しかし英語では、"I'm sorry." はお詫びの気持ちを表すので、使い方に注意しましょう。英語で謝意を表す場合は、"Thank you." が最もよく使われます。ちょっとしたことでもすぐに、笑顔で "Thank you." と言えるようにしましょう。

Reading

Read the following menu and select the best answer to each question.

BEST PIZZA Take-out OK. 10% discount on pick up orders.

Ingredients	Small	Medium	Large
All Meat	$8.00	$12.50	$17.00
Hawaiian	$7.00	$11.50	$16.00
Specialty Veggie	$7.50	$12.00	$16.50
Hot Mexican	$8.50	$13.00	$18.00

CALL 752-2222 Quick Free Delivery within Limited Areas

1. Which is the most expensive small pizza?

(A) All Meat

(B) Specialty Veggie

(C) Hot Mexican

2. Which pizza would be ordered by people who do not eat meat?

(A) Hawaiian

(B) Specialty Veggie

(C) Hot Mexican

3. How much would you pay when you take out a large Hot Mexican pizza?

(A) $16.20

(B) $16.70

(C) $18.00

4. Which of the following is TRUE?

(A) You can get a free pizza.

(B) You must carry the pizza out yourself.

(C) You can order pizza on the phone.

Pair Work

• •

Student A

Part I

You are visiting Wahoo Corporation. Using the pattern in **Model Conversation** (p. 44), talk to your partner who is the receptionist. Follow the instructions below and role play four times.

1. You are Mandy Smith from Bay Shore Hotel. You have an appointment with Mr. Robinson at 1:00. You would like to have coffee. You would like it black.

2. You are Chang Lee from China Corporation. You have an appointment with Ms. Frost at 1:45. You would like to have green tea.

3. You are Gina Rossi from XYZ Printing, Inc. You have an appointment with Ms. Collins at 3:15. You would like to have tea. You would like it with sugar and lemon.

4. You are Tom Hoffman from Sunlight Co., Ltd. You have an appointment with Ms. Yamada at 11:30. You would like to have apple juice.

Part II

You are a receptionist at Wahoo Corporation. Using the pattern in **Model Conversation** (p. 44), talk to your partner who is the visitor and complete the chart below. You will have four visitors.

Visitor	Appointment with...	Time	What he/she wants
Ex. Ken Adams	Mr. Yoshioka	2:30	tea (straight)

Student B

Part I

You are a receptionist at Wahoo Corporation. Using the pattern in **Model Conversation** (p. 44), talk to your partner who is the visitor and complete the chart below. You will have four visitors.

Visitor	Appointment with...	Time	What he/she wants
Ex. Ken Adams	Mr. Yoshioka	2:30	tea (straight)

Part II

You are visiting Wahoo Corporation. Using the pattern in **Model Conversation** (p. 44), talk to your partner who is the receptionist. Follow the instructions below and role play four times.

1. You are Sara Johnson from ABC Computing. You have an appointment with Mr. Hail at 3:00. You would like to have coffee. You would like it with sugar and cream.

2. You are Carlos Oliveira from Happy International Travel. You have an appointment with Ms. Sato at 10:30. You would like to have tea. You would like it straight.

3. You are Elena Gomez from Southeast Airlines. You have an appointment with Mr. Yoshioka at 9:45. You would like to have some water.

4. You are Tim Davis from Western Food Service. You have an appointment with Ms. Okada at 4:15. You would like to have orange juice.

Writing

38

Fill in the blanks with the appropriate words. Listen to the CD and check your answers.

Receptionist:	Hello. ( ) may I help you?
Man:	Hi. ( ) ( ) to see Mr. Davis of the Marketing ( ). I have an ( ) with him at 10:00.
Receptionist:	( ) I have your name?
Man:	Sure. I'm Carlos Oliveira from Happy International Travel.
Receptionist:	( ) this way, please. *(pause)* Mr. Davis will be here soon. ( ) ( ) ( ) something to drink while you are waiting? We ( ) coffee, tea and juice.
Man:	May I have a cup of coffee, please?
Receptionist:	Sure. *(pause)* ( ) you are.

Listening

Part I: Question and Response

Listen to the CD. You will hear a question or statement followed by three responses. Select the best response to the question or statement.

39
40

1. (A) (B) (C)   **2.** (A) (B) (C)

Part II: Short Conversation

Listen to the CD. You will hear a short conversation. Select the best answer to each question.

41

1. Where is this conversation most likely to take place?

(A) At a restaurant   (B) At a gym   (C) In a theater

2. What did the woman order?

(A) Tea with lemon and sugar

(B) Tea with milk

(C) Tea with milk and sugar

Unit 8

"Let's go out for a drink."

Invitation

Goal

Inviting someone to an activity and responding to an invitation

食事や催し物などへの誘い方、また誘われたとき
の返答について学びます

Key Expressions

Listen and repeat the following expressions.

1. Let's go out for a drink.
2. I'd love to go, but I have other plans.
3. How about Thursday evening?

Model Conversation

Practice the following dialogue with your partner.

A: Let's go out for a drink tomorrow   → go to the movie
night.

B: I'd love to go, but I have other plans.   → another appointment
Maybe some other time.

A: How about Thursday evening?

B: Sounds good.   → great

A: Why don't we meet at the station   → Shall we
around 6:00?

B: OK. See you then.

Class Work

Ask your partner to go out for a drink. Move around the class and practice the conversation. Write down the information in the chart.

Let's go out for a drink after the class.
I'd love to go, but I have other plans.

	Partner's name	Partner's response
Ex.	Miki Kishimoto	sounds good / has other plans (circled: has other plans)
		sounds good / has other plans
		sounds good / has other plans
		sounds good / has other plans
		sounds good / has other plans
		sounds good / has other plans
		sounds good / has other plans
		sounds good / has other plans

Cultural Tips

In some countries, people hold parties at home. For example, a potluck party is when each guest brings some food or drinks to share with everyone. A housewarming party is held when someone moves to a new place, and a baby shower is held before a woman gives birth. A bachelor party is for a single man just before he gets married. There are also birthday parties and farewell parties.

ホームパーティがよく開かれる国があります。参加者が1品ずつ食べ物や飲み物を持ち寄るpotluckと呼ばれるものや、引っ越し祝いのhousewarming、出産前に行うbaby shower、結婚前の独身男性のパーティであるbachelor party、さらにはbirthday partyやfarewell party（送別会）などがあります。

Reading

Read the following letter and select the best answer to each question. ●

September 3, 2012

Dear Ms. Yamada,

You are cordially invited to a reception to be held at the Bay Shore Hotel, Rose Ballroom on November 29, 2012 in honor of our 25th anniversary. Drinks will be served from 6:00 p.m., and dinner will start at 6:30 p.m. Please RSVP with the reply card by October 10.

Yours sincerely,

Mandy Smith

Mandy Smith

Manager, Bay Shore Hotel

1. What is enclosed with this letter?
   (A) A free drink coupon   (B) A hotel check in form   (C) A reply card

2. What is this letter?
   (A) A complaint   (B) An application   (C) An invitation

3. By when should the recipient respond to this letter?
   (A) By September 3   (B) By October 10   (C) By November 29

4. What will begin at 6:30?
   (A) The opening speech   (B) The meal   (C) The live concert

Pair Work

• •

Student A

Part I

Look at the planner below. You already have some plans for the weekend, but you want to spend some spare time with your partner. Using the pattern in **Model Conversation** (p. 50), talk to him/her and fix the following plans. Write down the new schedule in the planner.

1. go out for a drink / Friday night / meet at the station

2. play tennis / Saturday morning / meet in front of the park

Part II

Your partner wants to spend his/her spare time with you this weekend. Look at the planner below. You already have some plans. Using the pattern in **Model Conversation** (p. 50), talk to him/her. Write down the new schedule in the planner.

	Friday	Saturday	Sunday
9:00	9:00–12:00 work		
10:00			
11:00		11:30–1:30 lunch	
12:00		w/ Naoko; meet in front of Express Café	
1:00			
2:00			
3:00		3:00– gym	
4:00			
5:00			
6:00			
7:00			7:00– party at Ken's
8:00			w/ Sara; meet at the station
9:00			
10:00			

Part I

Your partner wants to spend his/her spare time with you this weekend. Look at the planner below. You already have some plans. Using the pattern in **Model Conversation** (p. 50), talk to him/her. Write down the new schedule in the planner.

Part II

Look at the planner below. You already have some plans for the weekend, but you want to spend some spare time with your partner. Using the pattern in **Model Conversation** (p. 50), talk to him/her and fix the following plans. Write down the new schedule in the planner.

1. go out for lunch / Saturday / meet at the station

2. go shopping / Saturday afternoon / meet at the shopping mall

	Friday	Saturday	Sunday
9:00		9:00–11:30 work	
10:00			
11:00	11:30–1:30 lunch		
12:00	w/ Miki; meet at the station		
1:00			
2:00			2:30–4:00 swimming
3:00			w/ Tom; meet in the lobby
4:00			
5:00			
6:00	6:00–9:00		
7:00	computer class		7:00– party at Ken's
8:00			w/ Sara; meet at the station
9:00			
10:00			

Writing

● ●○

You are organizing a farewell party for your colleague, Tina Collins.
Complete the following invitation using the information below.

Date:	September 28	RSVP:	by September 14
Place:	Lucianno's Italian Restaurant	Cost:	5,000 yen (includes a gift for Tina)
Purpose:	Tina's farewell party		

Dear all,

You are (   ) to (   ) (   )

(   ) to be held at (   ) (   )

(   ) on (   ) (   ) at 7:00 p.m. The

cost of the party is (   ) (   ) which includes a

(   ) for Tina. Please (   ) to me by

(   ) (   ).

Thank you.

(   ) (   )
your first name   *your last name*

Listening

● ●○

Part I: Question and Response

Listen to the CD. You will hear a question or statement followed by three
responses. Select the best response to the question or statement.

1. (A) (B) (C)   **2.** (A) (B) (C)

Part II: Short Talk

Listen to the CD. You will hear a short talk.
Select the best answer to each question.

1. When is the party?

(A) Tomorrow   (B) Thursday   (C) Saturday

2. Why is Beth planning a party for Scott?

(A) Because he got a promotion.   (B) Because he is leaving the company.

(C) Because he will be transferred to a different office.

"How was your weekend?"

Small Talk

Goal

Understanding what small talk is and enjoying it in various situations

英語特有のスモールトークを学び、会話を楽しみます

Key Expressions

Listen and repeat the following expressions. 47

1. How was your weekend?
2. How did you like the movie?
3. What do you do in your free time?

Model Conversation

Practice the following dialogue with your partner. 48

A: Hi, Naoko. How was your weekend?

B: Busy! I went shopping with my ► Great.
friends and saw a movie.

A: How did you like the movie? ► How was

B: It was great. What did you do over ► interesting
the weekend?

A: I stayed at home and relaxed, which
is not what I usually do.

B: Good for you. What do you usually ► That's nice.
do in your free time?

A: I like to exercise. I go to a gym
three times a week. ► almost every day

Class Work

• ▼

Talk about your weekend with your partner. Move around the class and practice the conversation. Write down the information in the chart.

How was your weekend?

That's nice.

Great. I _went shopping and ate out_.

Partner's name	What he/she did
Ex. Ken Adams	went shopping and ate out

🔅 Cultural Tips

You can easily make friends through small talk. It is important to listen and react to what you hear, and ask follow-up questions. You should also pay attention to facial expressions and gestures to keep the conversation moving smoothly. If you do not participate in the conversation actively, it will be harder for others to get to know you.

ちょっとした会話 (small talk) から、簡単に友情が芽生えることがあります。会話では、相づちやリアクションを大切にし、話題をふくらませていく努力をしましょう。また、表情やジェスチャーも会話をスムーズに進めるために重要な役割を果たしますので、注意しましょう。人見知りで積極的に会話に参加できないと、相手に自分のことを知ってもらうのが難しくなってしまいます。

Reading

Read the following letters and select the best answer to each question.

September 5, 2012

Dear Ms. Smith,

I appreciate the invitation to
the reception. I would be very
happy to attend this event at
the Bay Shore Hotel. I'm looking
forward to it.

Best regards,

Naoko Yamada

Naoko Yamada

September 7, 2012

Dear Ms. Smith,

I was very pleased to be invited
to the reception to be held at
the Bay Shore Hotel. However,
I'm afraid I will be unable to
attend because I have another
appointment. I'm sure this will
be a great event for everyone
who participates.

I wish you all the best.

Yours truly,

Scott Robinson

Scott Robinson

1. Who is going to attend the reception?

(A) Ms. Yamada   (B) Mr. Robinson   (C) Ms. Yamada and Mr. Robinson

2. Who is organizing the reception?

(A) Ms. Yamada   (B) Mr. Robinson   (C) Ms. Smith

3. Why is Mr. Robinson unable to attend the reception?

(A) Because he has something else to do.

(B) Because he has not made an appointment.

(C) Because he has never stayed at the hotel.

4. Which of the following is TRUE?

(A) Neither Ms. Yamada nor Mr. Robinson is excited about the reception.

(B) Both Ms. Yamada and Mr. Robinson are happy to be invited.

(C) Both Ms. Yamada and Mr. Robinson are going to the reception.

Pair Work

··· •

Student A

1. Practice making small talk. Ask your partner question #1 in the chart below and write down his/her answer. Then, make as many follow-up questions as possible. Count how many follow-up questions you ask and write the number in the chart.

2. Your partner will ask you a question. Answer the question briefly. Keep the conversation as your partner continues asking questions.

3. Take turns with your partner and complete the chart.

Ex. **A:** What do you usually do in your free time? [First Question]
      B: I like to exercise.
      A: How often do you exercise? [Follow-up question]
      B: Maybe three times a week.
      A: Do you go to a gym? [Follow-up question]
      B: Yes. I go to Let's Workout.
      A: How much do you pay each month? [Follow-up question]
      B: About 8,000 yen.

	First Question	Partner's answer	Number of follow-up question(s)
Ex.	What do you usually do in your free time?	I like to exercise.	3
1	What do you usually do in your free time?		
2	How was your weekend?		
3	Do you like movies?		
4	What did you eat this morning?		
5	*Your original question* ( )		

Student B

1. Practice making small talk. Your partner will ask you a question. Answer the question briefly. Keep the conversation as your partner continues asking questions.

2. Ask your partner question #1 in the chart below and write down his/her answer. Then, make as many follow-up questions as possible. Count how many follow-up questions you ask and write the number in the chart.

3. Take turns with your partner and complete the chart.

Ex. **A:** Do you play any sports? [First Question]
  B: No, I don't.
  A: Did you play any sports when you were a student? [Follow-up question]
  B: Yes. I played softball.
  A: Really? What position did you play? [Follow-up question]
  B: Catcher.

	First Question	Partner's answer	Number of follow-up question(s)
Ex.	*Do you play any sports?*	*No, I don't.*	*2*
1	Do you play any sports?		
2	How do you like your school/work?		
3	It's a beautiful day, isn't it?		
4	How was your dinner yesterday?		
5	*Your original question* ( )		

Writing

• ▼

You are invited to a farewell party for one of your colleagues, Tina Collins.
Complete the following letter of acceptance.

```
Dear Mike,

(              ) (                              ) the invitation to
(              ) (                    ) (                    ).
I (          ) (                ) (                )
(              ) to attend this event at Lucianno's Italian
Restaurant. I (                ) (                )
(              ) to it.


Best regards,

(              ) (                    )
    your first name          your last name
```

Listening

• ▼

Part I: Question and Response

Listen to the CD. You will hear a question or statement followed by three
responses. Select the best response to the question or statement.

1. (A) (B) (C)   **2.** (A) (B) (C)

Part II: Short Conversation

Listen to the CD. You will hear a short conversation.
Select the best answer to each question.

1. What did the man do on the weekend?

(A) He ate out.   (B) He went to Tokyo.   (C) He relaxed at home.

2. What may they do next weekend?

(A) They will work together.   (B) They will go out for dinner.

(C) They will relax at home.

"The sales department is on the 3rd floor."

Location

Goal

Explaining and asking for locations

位置や場所を尋ねたり、説明したりします

Key Expressions

Listen and repeat the following expressions.

🔽 52

1. The sales department is on the 3rd floor.
2. The men's room is to the left of the vending machine.
3. The conference room is across from the elevator.

Model Conversation

Practice the following dialogue with your partner.

🔽 53

A: Could you tell me where the
   sales department is? → conference room
B: Of course. It's on the 3rd floor,
   to the left of the copy room. → right
   Please take the elevator. → stairs
A: Thank you. Oh, where can I find
   the elevator? → stairs
B: It's next to the restroom.
A: Thanks for your help.

Class Work

Choose one name of the place from the box to make a question. Respond to the question as you like. Move around the class and practice the conversation. Write down the names of the places on the building layout.

Where is the _cafeteria_ ?

It's on the _4th_ floor.

cafeteria
restroom
reception
sales department
conference room
copy room

Thank you.

No problem.

	5F	
Ex. Cafeteria	4F	
	3F	
	2F	
	1F	

Reading

Read the following e-mail and select the best answer to each question.

Sent: September 21, 14:00
From: tyoshioka@wahoo.co.jp
To: srobinson@wahoo.co.jp; nyamada@wahoo.co.jp
Re: Notice of October 1 meeting

Hi everyone,

I'd like to let you know that there will be a meeting on October 1 at 2:00 in the conference room.

The conference room is in the new building. It's on the 5th floor, to the right of the staff lounge, between the staff lounge and the supply room.

If you can't come, please let me know ASAP.

Thanks,
Toshi Yoshioka

---

1. Why was this e-mail sent?
(A) To announce a meeting   (B) To cancel a meeting
(C) To arrange a meeting

2. Where is the conference room?
(A) It is on the 1st floor.   (B) It is behind the staff lounge.
(C) It is to the left of the supply room.

3. When will the meeting start?
(A) At 2:00 on September 21   (B) At 2:00 on the first day of October
(C) As early as possible on the 5th

4. What should you do if you can't attend the meeting?
(A) Contact Toshi quickly   (B) Ask to change the meeting time
(C) Go to the conference room immediately

Pair Work

•• ⓥ

Student A

Part I

Learn the following vocabulary used in offices.
Listen to the CD and check the pronunciation.

staff lounge	personnel department
cafeteria	sales department
information systems department	public relations department
customer service department	supply room
marketing department	copy room
accounting department	conference room

Part II

Look at the map. You are at the reception of Wahoo Corporation. You want to know where the following places are. Ask your partner by using the pattern in **Model Conversation** (p. 62) and write down the names of the places in the map. You make a question first. Then, take turns with your partner.

1. Staff Lounge
2. Sales Department
3. Conference Room
4. Customer Service Department
5. Accounting Department

Wahoo Corporation

Women's Room		Cafeteria			Copy Room	Supply Room		Men's Room
Women's Room	STAIRS	Public Relations Department			Marketing Department		ELEVATOR	Men's Room
Women's Room				Personnel Department		Information Systems Department		Men's Room
Women's Room		Reception						Men's Room

Part I

Learn the following vocabulary used in offices.
Listen to the CD and check the pronunciation. 54

staff lounge	personnel department
cafeteria	sales department
information systems department	public relations department
customer service department	supply room
marketing department	copy room
accounting department	conference room

Part II

Look at the map. You are at the reception of Wahoo Corporation. You want to
know where the following places are. Ask your partner by using the pattern in
Model Conversation (p. 62) and write down the names of the places in the map.
Your partner makes a question first. Then, take turns with your partner.

1. Cafeteria
2. Copy Room
3. Marketing Department
4. Public Relations Department
5. Personnel Department

Wahoo Corporation

Women's Room	STAIRS		Conference Room				Supply Room	ELEVATOR	Men's Room
Women's Room				Customer Service Department			Staff Lounge		Men's Room
Women's Room		Accounting Department				Sales Department	Information Systems Department		Men's Room
Women's Room				Reception					Men's Room

Writing

•••○

Look at the map in **Pair Work** (p. 66). You are going to have a staff meeting on October 17, at 3:30 p.m. It is going to be held in the sales department. Complete the following e-mail message to staff members to let them know when and where the meeting is going to take place.

Dear all,

(   ) (   ) (   ) let you know that (   )
will be a (   ) (   ) on (   ) (   ) at
(   ) (   ) in the (   ) (   ).

The (   ) (   ) is on the (   ) floor, (   ) the
(   ) (   ) and the (   ) (   ) (   ).

If you can't (   ), please let me know (   ).

Regards,

(   ) (   )
   your first name   *your last name*

Listening

•••○

Part I: Question and Response

Listen to the CD. You will hear a question or statement followed by three responses. Select the best response to the question or statement. 55 56

1. (A) (B) (C)   **2.** (A) (B) (C)

Part II: Short Talk

Listen to the CD. You will hear a short talk.
Select the best answer to each question. 57

1. Where would you hear this announcement?

    (A) At a department store   (B) At the company   (C) At the airport

2. Which of the following is TRUE?

    (A) There is a cafeteria on the 5th floor.

    (B) A copy room is next to the sales department.

    (C) A staff lounge is on the 1st floor.

Unit 11

"Turn right on Main Street."

Directions

Goal
Giving and asking for directions

道順を尋ねたり、説明したりします

Key Expressions

Listen and repeat the following expressions. 58

1. Could you tell me how to get to your office?
2. Turn right on Main Street.
3. Go straight for three blocks.

Model Conversation

Practice the following dialogue with your partner. 59

A: Could you tell me how to get to your office? ► How do I

B: Sure. Go out Exit 5 at Central Station. ► Certainly.
Then, go straight for three blocks. Then, turn
right on Main Street. ► left

A: OK. Go straight for three blocks and turn
right. ► left

B: That's right.

A: And then?

B: You will see our office on your left, across ► right
from the bank.

A: Thanks a lot.

Class Work

• ▼

Choose one name of the place from the box to make a question. Respond to the question as you like. Move around the class and practice the conversation. Write down the names of the places on the map.

Could you tell me how to get to _ABA Hotel_ ?

Sure. Go straight for _3_ blocks. It's on your _left_.

ABA Hotel
post office
bank
high school
library
supermarket
coffee shop

Ex. ABA Hotel	

Where You Are Now

Cultural Tips

In Japan, people say traffic lights are red, blue, and yellow while in some countries, people say green instead of blue. Jaywalking is a serious crime in some countries, so always use the pedestrian crossing when you are abroad. The address system in Japan uses area and block names. In the U.S., a system of street names and numbers is used. Odd numbers are given on one side of the street while even numbers are given on the other side of the street. There are some very long streets which have over 1,000 address numbers in the U.S.

日本では信号は赤・青・黄ですが、青ではなく、緑と言う国もあります。交通規制を無視し、歩道でないところを渡ることが重い罪になる国もありますので、必ず横断歩道を渡るようにしましょう。また、アメリカでは、ある区画を「町」とするのではなく、道路単位で住所を表記します。そのため、アメリカでは、すべての通りに名前がついています。道路の片側が偶数番地で、反対側が奇数番地になっていて、1000番地を越えるような長い通りもあります。

Reading

Read the following fax and select the best answer to each question.

FAX

HAPPY INTERNATIONAL TRAVEL
419 Manhattan Street, New York,
NY 10010 USA
Tel No: +1-212-151-2255
Fax No: +1-212-151-2256

To: Mr. Toshi Yoshioka

From: Carlos Oliveira

Tel No: +81-6-8798-0200   Pages: 2 (including this coversheet)

Fax No: +81-6-8798-0100   Date: November 5, 2012

Re: Directions to our office

Dear Mr. Yoshioka,

I'm sending a map to help you to get to our office. You can also visit our website.

After going out Exit 8, turn right on Manhattan Street. Go straight for five blocks and you'll see the police station on your left. Our office is to the right of the police station.

It's about a 10-minute walk from the station. If you have any trouble getting here, give us a call. We're looking forward to seeing you then.

Carlos Oliveira
Carlos Oliveira

---

1. What was sent with this message?

(A) Nothing   (B) A company brochure   (C) A map

2. What should Mr. Yoshioka do after leaving the exit?

(A) Go straight for five blocks   (B) Turn right on Manhattan Street
(C) Make a phone call

3. Which of the following is TRUE?

(A) The office is across from the police station.

(B) It takes about 10 minutes on foot to get to the office.

(C) The office is difficult to find.

4. What should Mr. Yoshioka do if he has difficulty finding the office?

(A) Call their office   (B) Visit their website   (C) Take a taxi from the station

Pair Work

● ●

Student A

Look at the map. You are at Central Station. You want to know how to get to the following places. Ask your partner by using the pattern in **Model Conversation** (p. 68) and write down the names of the places in the map. You make a question first. Then, take turns with your partner.

1. Joe's Seafood House
2. City Hall
3. City Library
4. ABA Hotel
5. Auto Best

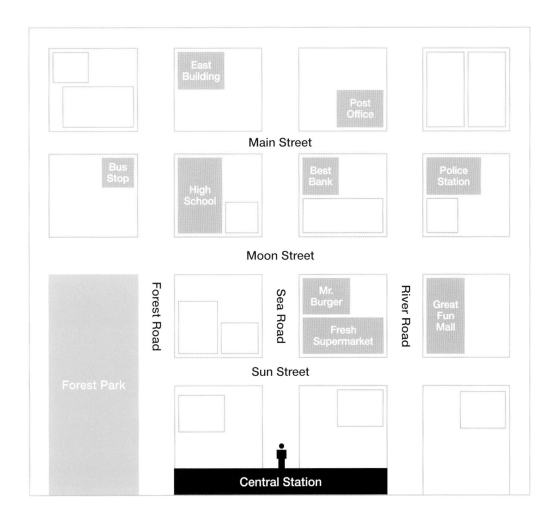

Look at the map. You are at Central Station. You want to know how to get to the following places. Ask your partner by using the pattern in **Model Conversation** (p. 68) and write down the names of the places in the map. Your partner makes a question first. Then, take turns with your partner.

1. Great Fun Mall
2. Post Office
3. High School
4. Best Bank
5. East Building

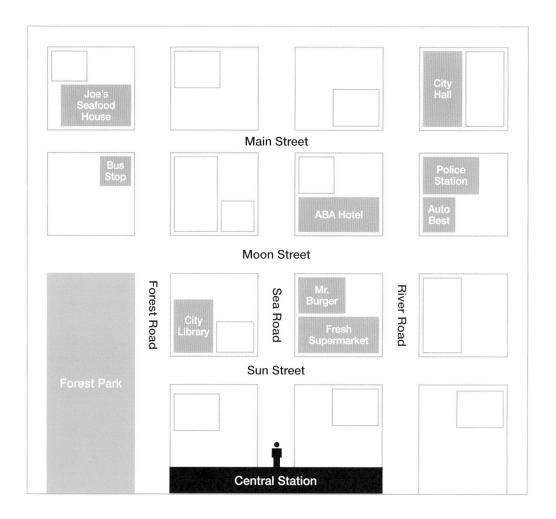

Writing

•••○

Look at the map in **Pair Work** (p. 72) and complete the following directions from Central Station to the police station.

> After (   ) (   ) Exit 5 at (   ) (   ),
>
> go (   ) for (   ) blocks and turn (   ) on
>
> (   ) Street. Go straight for (   ) blocks and you'll
>
> (   ) the (   ) (   ) on your (   ).

Listening

•••○

Part I: Question and Response

Listen to the CD. You will hear a question or statement followed by three responses. Select the best response to the question or statement.

1. (A) (B) (C)   **2.** (A) (B) (C)

Part II: Short Conversation

Listen to the CD. You will hear a short conversation.
Select the best answer to each question.

1. Why did Mr. Hoffman call?

    (A) Because he was late for work.

    (B) Because he was lost.

    (C) Because he got to the station.

2. Which of the following is TRUE?

    (A) He is quite far from the office.

    (B) He went out of the west exit.

    (C) He sees the bank on his right.

"First, press the start button."

Instructions

Key Expressions

● 63

Listen and repeat the following expressions.

1. First, press the start button.
2. Next, open the tray.
3. Finally, put in a CD.

Model Conversation

● 64

Practice the following dialogue with your partner.

A: Could you show me how to change the ink cartridge?

B: Sure. First, open the cover.   ⊢ lift the lid

A: Uh huh.

B: Next, take out the old ink cartridge.

A: OK.

B: Snap the new one into place.   ⊢ Put

A: And then?

B: Finally, check that the icon changes to   ⊢ see if
"READY."

A: Hmm…, it's easier than I thought. Thank   ⊢ more difficult
you very much.

Class Work

Choose one item from the box to make a question. Respond to the question by using "open the tray" or "press the start button." Move around the class and practice the conversation. Write down the information in the chart.

Could you tell me how to use a **DVD player** ?

Sure. First, **open the tray** .

DVD player
CD player
printer
computer
scanner
coffee maker
copy machine
digital camera

Partner's name	Item	First step
Ex. *Toshi Yoshioka*	*DVD player*	(open the tray) / press the start button
		open the tray / press the start button
		open the tray / press the start button
		open the tray / press the start button
		open the tray / press the start button
		open the tray / press the start button
		open the tray / press the start button
		open the tray / press the start button

🔆 Cultural Tips

Various countries use different electrical voltages and outlets. When traveling abroad or inviting overseas guests, make sure the electrical equipment and the local power are compatible. You or your guest may need to use adapters or small transformers in order to use hair driers, chargers, or computers.

国によって使用する電圧やプラグは異なります。海外旅行の際や、海外から人が来る場合は、電化製品の互換性やその国で使えるものについて、しっかり確認しておいたほうがよいでしょう。場合によっては、ドライヤーや充電池、パソコンなどを使うためにアダプターや変圧器が必要なことがあります。

Reading

Read the following article and select the best answer to each question.

How to Print Pictures with a PC

You can print your pictures by following a few simple instructions:
First, connect your camera to your computer. Usually you will use a USB cable to do so. Next, choose where you want your pictures to be downloaded, such as "My Documents" or a USB memory device. After downloading the pictures from the camera, choose the pictures you want to print. Finally, click on the printer icon.

If you have any questions, feel free to e-mail us.

1. What is this article about?
(A) How to take pictures
(B) How to use a camera
(C) How to print photos

2. How many steps are there?
(A) Three
(B) Five
(C) Seven

3. What is the first step?
(A) Take pictures with a camera
(B) Connect your camera to your computer
(C) Choose the pictures you want

4. What is most likely to be used to connect your camera to a PC?
(A) A USB cable
(B) A USB memory device
(C) My Documents

Pair Work

Student A

You want to know how to use the following items. Ask your partner by using the pattern in **Model Conversation** (p. 74) and fill in the blanks. You make a question first. Then, take turns with your partner.

1. a fax machine   **2.** a coffee maker   **3.** a copy machine

Item	Instructions
a fax machine	First, put in the ( ). Next, ( ) the fax number. Then, listen for the ( ) ( ). Finally, ( ) the start button.
a scanner	First, open the cover. Next, place the paper facedown. Then, close the cover. Finally, press the start button.
a coffee maker	First, put in the ( ). Next, ( ) a filter in the maker. Then, put ( ) into the filter. Finally, ( ) the start button.
a CD player	First, open the tray. Next, put in a CD. Then, close the tray. Finally, press the play button.
a copy machine	First, ( ) the cover. Next, ( ) the paper facedown and close the ( ). Then, ( ) how many copies you want. Finally, press the ( ) button.
a printer	First, put in the paper. Next, open the document you want to print. Then, choose how many copies you want. Finally, click on the printer icon.

Student B

You want to know how to use the following items. Ask your partner by using the pattern in **Model Conversation** (p. 74) and fill in the blanks. Your partner makes a question first. Then, take turns with your partner.

1. a scanner   **2.** a CD player   **3.** a printer

Item	Instructions
a fax machine	First, put in the paper. Next, dial the fax number. Then, listen for the fax tone. Finally, press the start button.
a scanner	First, open the ( ). Next, ( ) the paper facedown. Then, ( ) the cover. Finally, press the ( ) button.
a coffee maker	First, put in the water. Next, put a filter in the maker. Then, put coffee into the filter. Finally, press the start button.
a CD player	First, ( ) the tray. Next, ( ) ( ) a CD. Then, close the ( ). Finally, press the play ( ).
a copy machine	First, open the cover. Next, place the paper facedown and close the cover. Then, choose how many copies you want. Finally, press the start button.
a printer	First, put in the ( ). Next, open the ( ) you want to ( ). Then, ( ) how many copies you want. Finally, ( ) on the printer icon.

Writing

•• ▼

Use the statements in the box below to write a short explanation about how to buy a train ticket in Japan. Use "first," "next," "then," and "finally" accordingly.

Insert money into the machine.   Take your ticket.
Don't forget to take your change.   Find the price.
Select the price you want.   Decide where you want to go.

How to buy a train ticket in Japan

Listening

•• ▼

Part I: Question and Response

Listen to the CD. You will hear a question or statement followed by three responses. Select the best response to the question or statement.

1. (A) (B) (C)   **2.** (A) (B) (C)

Part II: Short Talk

Listen to the CD. You will hear a short talk.
Select the best answer to each question.

1. What is the speaker talking about?

(A) How to use a credit card

(B) How to cash a check

(C) How to withdraw money

2. What should you do first?

(A) Put in the card   (B) Enter the number   (C) Select "withdraw cash"

13 "I'd like to check in."

Checking in at a Hotel

⚑ Goal

Checking in at a hotel

ホテルでのチェックイン
時の会話を練習します

Key Expressions

Listen and repeat the following expressions. ●–V 🎧 68

1. I'd like to check in.
2. You'll be staying for three nights, right?
3. How would you like to pay?

Model Conversation

Practice the following dialogue with your partner. ●–V 🎧 69

A: Hi, I'd like to check in. I have a reservation.

B: <u>May I have</u> your name, please? ⟶ Could you give me

A: Sure. My name is Toshi Yoshioka.

B: Yes, Mr. Yoshioka. You'll be staying for three nights, right?

A: <u>Yes.</u> ⟶ Exactly.

B: And, you would like a <u>single non-smoking</u> room? ⟶ double smoking

A: That's right.

B: How would you like to pay?

A: By <u>credit card</u>. Here you are. ⟶ traveler's check

B: OK. *(pause)* Could you sign your name here?

A: Sure. *(pause)* Here you go.

B: Thank you, sir.

Class Work

Choose "credit card" or "traveler's check" for your response. Move around the class and practice the conversation. Write down the information and have your partner sign his/her name in the chart.

How would you like to pay?

Could you sign your name here?

By _credit card_ , please.

Partner's name	Payment method	Signature
Ex. Naoko Yamada	credit card / traveler's check	Naoko Yamada
	credit card / traveler's check	
	credit card / traveler's check	
	credit card / traveler's check	
	credit card / traveler's check	
	credit card / traveler's check	
	credit card / traveler's check	
	credit card / traveler's check	

⌾ Cultural Tips

You might be worried about cash being stolen or lost, especially when you travel overseas. Traveler's checks are very useful, as well as credit cards. However, you need to pay some extra fees when you use a traveler's check. A lost traveler's check can be replaced by following the appropriate procedure. In North America, many people use personal checks to pay for things. A personal check is one way of withdrawing money directly from your bank account.

海外渡航中には、現金の盗難や紛失が心配されます。海外旅行ではクレジットカードだけでなく、トラベラーズチェック（旅行小切手）も便利です。発行には手数料がかかりますが、盗難や紛失の際に再発行してもらうことができます。また北米では、日常生活においても個人が支払いにチェック（小切手）を用いることが多く、こちらは personal check と呼ばれます。personal check は自分の銀行口座から直接引き落とされることになっています。

Reading

Read the following form and select the best answer to each question.

Bay Shore Hotel

110 Main Street, Exeter, NH
(603) 715-8800
www.bayshore.com

Name: Naoko Yamada

Street address: 6-29-3 Umeda, Kita-ku

City: Osaka

State: Osaka, Japan   Zip code: 530-0001

Expected Arrival Time: 8:00 pm

Mon. Tues. Wed. Thur. Fri. Sat. Sun.

Date: November 28, 2012

No. of guests: 1

No. of rooms: 1

Room no.: 803

Room rate: $120

No. of nights: 3

Subtotal: $360

Sales tax 5.5%: $19.80

Total charge: $379.80

Paid by: Cash / Check / Credit Card

Date paid: December 1, 2012

1. How long did Ms. Yamada stay at this hotel?

(A) One night   (B) Two nights   (C) Three nights

2. How much was the room charge per night?

(A) $120   (B) $139.80   (C) $360

3. When did Ms. Yamada check out of the hotel?

(A) November 28, 2012   (B) November 30, 2012   (C) December 1, 2012

4. How did Ms. Yamada pay?

(A) By cash   (B) By credit card   (C) By traveler's check

Pair Work

Student A

Part I

You are a guest for the Sun Hotel and your partner is the clerk. Using the pattern in **Model Conversation** (p. 80), talk to him/her. You are going to stay for two nights in a single smoking room. You want to pay by traveler's check.

Part II

You are a clerk at the Star Hotel and your partner is the guest. He/She is supposed to stay for five nights in a double non-smoking room. Today is August 9. Using the pattern in **Model Conversation** (p. 80), talk to him/her and fill out the guest form below.

Star Hotel

1101 Central Avenue, Arlington, MA
(605) 248-1000
www.starhotel.com

**GUEST CHECK IN FORM
PLEASE PRINT**

NAME: MR./MS. _____ _____
                       Last   First

ADDRESS:

3-6-44 Satsuki, Higashi-ku
Street

Osaka   Osaka   Japan   530-0002
City   State   Country   Zip code

ARRIVAL DATE: _____

DEPARTURE DATE: _____

NO. OF NIGHTS: _____

ROOM TYPE: ☐ Single ☐ Double
              ☐ Smoking ☐ Non-smoking

METHOD OF PAYMENT:
              ☐ Cash ☐ Check ☐ Credit Card

Part I

You are a clerk at the Sun Hotel and your partner is the guest. He/She is supposed to stay for two nights in a single smoking room. Today is September 22. Using the pattern in **Model Conversation** (p. 80), talk to him/her and fill out the guest form below.

Sun Hotel

2810 Main Street, Milford, WA
(310) 255-8888
www.sunhotel.com

GUEST CHECK IN FORM
PLEASE PRINT

NAME: MR./MS. _____ _____
                         Last   First

ADDRESS:

2-7-4 Yamane-cho
_____
Street

Higashi-Tokyo   Tokyo   Japan   202-0006
City   State   Country   Zip code

ARRIVAL DATE: _____

DEPARTURE DATE: _____

NO. OF NIGHTS: _____

ROOM TYPE: ☐ Single ☐ Double
                ☐ Smoking ☐ Non-smoking

METHOD OF PAYMENT:
                ☐ Cash ☐ Check ☐ Credit Card

Part II

You are a guest for the Star Hotel and your partner is the clerk. Using the pattern in **Model Conversation** (p. 80), talk to him/her. You are going to stay for five nights in a double non-smoking room. You want to pay by credit card.

Writing

• ▼

Fill out the following check in form. The arrival date is today. You would like to stay in a single non-smoking room for five nights and pay by cash. For the other parts, use your real information.

Moon Hotel
562 Manhattan Street, New York, NY
(212) 151-9500
www.moonhotel.com

GUEST CHECK IN FORM
PLEASE PRINT

NAME: MR./MS. _____   _____
                          Last   First

ADDRESS: _____
                Street

          _____
                City   State   Country   Zip code

ARRIVAL DATE: _____   DEPARTURE DATE: _____

NO. OF NIGHTS: _____

ROOM TYPE: ☐ Single ☐ Double ☐ Smoking ☐ Non-smoking

METHOD OF PAYMENT: ☐ Cash ☐ Check ☐ Credit Card

Listening

• ▼

Part I: Question and Response

Listen to the CD. You will hear a question or statement followed by three responses. Select the best response to the question or statement.

1. (A) (B) (C)   **2.** (A) (B) (C)

Part II: Short Conversation

Listen to the CD. You will hear a short conversation.
Select the best answer to each question.

1. How would the woman like to pay?

(A) By cash   (B) By credit card   (C) By traveler's check

2. Why does the woman need to fill out the form?

(A) To cash a check   (B) To check out   (C) To place an order

"I'm looking for a souvenir."

Shopping

Goal

Asking for prices and other information when shopping

出張先でのショッピング時の会話や、商品や値段についての質問の仕方を学びます

Key Expressions

Listen and repeat the following expressions.

73

1. I'm looking for a souvenir.
2. How much is that?
3. Do you have it in another color?

Model Conversation

Practice the following dialogues with your partner.

74
75

1. **A:** Hello. <u>May I help you?</u> ----→ Can I help you?
   B: No, thank you. I'm just looking.

2. **A:** Hello. <u>May I help you?</u> ----→ Can I help you?
   B: Yes. I'm looking for a souvenir for my colleague in Japan.
   A: OK. How about this T-shirt? It's very popular.
   B: How much is that?
   A: Twelve dollars.
   B: OK. Do you have it in <u>another color</u>? ----→ a different size
   A: Certainly. We have <u>red, blue, and brown</u>. ----→ small, medium, and large
   B: OK. I'll take a <u>red</u> one. ----→ medium

Class Work

· ▼

Choose one item from the box to make a question. Respond to the question as you like. Move around the class and practice the conversation. Write down the information in the chart.

How much is this ___pen___ ?

It's _1 dollar and 50 cents_ .

pen
T-shirt
notebook
wine
watch

Partner's name	Item	Price
Ex. Toshi Yoshioka	pen	1 dollar and 50 cents

🔆 Cultural Tips

Some people think they must ask for a discount in all foreign countries. If there is a price tag, you are not supposed to ask for one unless the product has a defect. If you have a receipt, you can exchange the item or get a refund more easily than in Japan. However, most stores have a time limit for exchanging goods. For example, stores have a seven-day or 90-day time limit for getting refunds.

外国では「値切りが基本」と思っている人もいるかもしれませんが、価格表示のあるものは値切らないのが基本です。レシートがあれば、返品や交換は日本よりも気軽に応じてもらえます。ただし、ほとんどの店では、返品や交換期間が1週間あるいは90日などと決められています。

Reading

Read the following form and select the best answer to each question.

```
        KEN ADAMS          09/15                                    262
        469 CENTRAL AVENUE
        NEW YORK, NY 10010              Date  12/02/12              54-153/114
                                                                        442

Pay to the     Great Fun Mall                              $   252.60 —
order of _____

two hundred and fifty two dollars and sixty cents
_____

BB BEST BANK
   New York


For   leather bag                           Ken Adams
   _____              _____
```

1. What is the form called?

(A) A check

(B) A boarding pass

(C) A receipt

2. When was the form written?

(A) September 15, 2012

(B) February 6, 2002

(C) December 2, 2012

3. Who will receive the form?

(A) Ken Adams

(B) Great Fun Mall

(C) New York

4. Who filled in this form?

(A) Ken Adams

(B) Great Fun Mall

(C) Best Bank

Pair Work

● ●

Student A

Part I

You are a clerk at a duty-free store and your partner is the customer. Look at the list below. Using the pattern in **Model Conversation 2** (p. 86), take care of him/her.

Item	Price	Color	Size
tie	$25.00	yellow, blue, green	—
watch	¥12,000	silver, black	—
cap	$8.50	white, red, brown	small, medium, large
wine	¥2,500	—	—
coffee	$11.00	—	—

Part II

You are a customer at a duty-free store and your partner is the clerk. Using the pattern in **Model Conversation 2** (p. 86), ask him/her about the following items and fill in the blanks.

Item	Price	Color	Size
scarf			—
pen			—
sweat shirt			
perfume		—	—
bag		—	—

Student B

Part I

You are a customer at a duty-free store and your partner is the clerk. Using the pattern in **Model Conversation 2** (p. 86), ask him/her about the following items and fill in the blanks.

Item	Price	Color	Size
tie			—
watch			—
cap			
wine		—	—
coffee		—	—

Part II

You are a clerk at a duty-free store and your partner is the customer. Look at the list below. Using the pattern in **Model Conversation 2** (p. 86), take care of him/her.

Item	Price	Color	Size
scarf	$32.00	white, pink, red	—
pen	¥310	black, blue	—
sweat shirt	$19.50	white, gray, brown	extra small, medium, large
perfume	¥1,200	—	—
bag	$115.00	—	—

Writing

First, write your name and address on the upper left part of the check.
Now, you want to buy a coat at Best Mall. It costs $125.80. Fill in the
blanks and sign the check.

263

54-153/114
442

_____

_____

_____   Date _____

Pay to the
order of _____ $ [   ]

BB BEST BANK
    New York

For _____   _____

Listening

Part I: Question and Response

Listen to the CD. You will hear a question or statement followed by three
responses. Select the best response to the question or statement.

76
77

1. (A) (B) (C)   **2.** (A) (B) (C)

Part II: Short Talk

Listen to the CD. You will hear a short talk.
Select the best answer to each question.

78

1. What is being advertised?
   (A) A laptop computer   (B) A desktop computer   (C) A newest mobile phone

2. How much will this item cost?
   (A) $720   (B) $880   (C) $900

"What would you like to have?"

Eating out

Key Expressions

Listen and repeat the following expressions. 79

1. What would you like to have?
2. I'll have a cheeseburger with a garden salad.
3. Shall we order some dessert?

Model Conversation

Practice the following dialogue with your partner. 80

A: What would you like to have, Naoko? ⟶ order

B: Well, I'll have a cheeseburger with a garden salad. How about you, Scott?

A: Uh, I'll have a chicken burger with some soup.

B: What would you like to drink?

A: I'll have coffee after the meal. ⟶ before

B: OK. Shall we order some dessert? ⟶ Why don't we

A: Sure. I'd like to try the fresh fruit ice cream.

Class Work

· ▼

Choose one item from the box for your response. Move around the class and practice the conversation. Write down the information in the chart.

What would you like to have?

I'll have a ___salad___.

salad
burger
pasta
steak
pizza

Partner's name	Partner's order
Ex. Toshi Yoshioka	salad

💡 Cultural Tips

In North America, one server may serve just one table. Usually, you pay a 10% to 20% tip to your server. Tips are part of a server's salary, so do not forget to leave them. You can pay a tip in cash by leaving it on the table when you leave, or add it on the credit card form. Decide how much of a tip to leave according to the quality of the service.

北米のレストランなどでは1つのテーブルを1人の店員が担当することが多く、客は最後に、食事代の10～20%をチップとして支払うのが一般的です。チップは店員の給料でもあるため、忘れないようにしましょう。チップは現金をテーブルに置いていってもよいし、クレジットカードで支払うこともできます。チップをいくらにするかは、店員のサービスの質で決めるとよいでしょう。

Reading

Read the following menu and select the best answer to each question.

Cafeteria Menu

BURGERS

Burger	$4.00
Cheeseburger	$5.00
Bacon cheeseburger	$6.50
Chicken burger	$5.25
BBQ beef burger	$6.00

served with French fries or green salad

SALADS

Green salad	$2.00
Chef's salad	$3.00
Garden salad	$2.50

SOUPS

Soup of the day	$2.00
Corn chowder	$2.00
Clam chowder	$3.50

BEVERAGES

Coffee/Tea	$1.00
Soda	$1.20

DESSERTS

Ice cream	$2.00
Cake (chocolate/cheese)	$3.50

1. What will be included if you order a bacon cheeseburger?

(A) Soup of the day   (B) Coffee   (C) French fries

2. What is "Soup of the day"?

(A) It is the day everyone gets free soup.

(B) It is soup you eat every day.

(C) It is the kind of soup that is different each day.

3. What is one kind of cake that is available?

(A) Chocolate   (B) Ice cream   (C) White cream

4. Which of the following is TRUE?

(A) There are five kinds of burgers at the cafeteria.

(B) A green salad is served with French fries.

(C) The BBQ beef burger is the most expensive item on the menu.

Pair Work

Student A

Part I

1. You are at a restaurant with your colleague. Using the pattern in **Model Conversation** (p. 92), talk about your own order. You start the conversation.

2. Now, your partner starts the conversation. Write down your partner's order in the chart below.

Part II

Change partners and repeat the tasks above.

MENU

SOUPS and SALADS

Greek salad	$6.50
Caesar salad	$8.25
Taco beef salad	$9.50
Soup of the day	$4.50
Vegetable soup	$5.50

PASTA

Lasagna	$11.50
Spaghetti w/ meat sauce	$11.50
Macaroni w/ cream sauce	$11.00

Served w/ garlic toast and Caesar salad

STEAKS and SEAFOOD

Hunter steak	$14.95
Salmon steak	$16.95
Sirloin steak	$18.95

Served w/ fries and soup or salad

BEVERAGES and DESSERTS

Coffee/Tea	$2.50
Soda	$2.00
Ice cream	$3.00
Cake	$4.25

Partner's name	Order
Ex. Ken Adams	Salmon steak, Caesar salad, Coffee, Ice cream

95

Part I

1. You are at a restaurant with your colleague. Using the pattern in **Model Conversation** (p. 92), talk about your own order. Your partner starts the conversation. Write down your partner's order in the chart below.

2. Now, you start the conversation.

Part II

Change partners and repeat the tasks above.

MENU

SOUPS and SALADS

Greek salad	$6.50
Caesar salad	$8.25
Taco beef salad	$9.50
Soup of the day	$4.50
Vegetable soup	$5.50

PASTA

Lasagna	$11.50
Spaghetti w/ meat sauce	$11.50
Macaroni w/ cream sauce	$11.00

Served w/ garlic toast and Caesar salad

STEAKS and SEAFOOD

Hunter steak	$14.95
Salmon steak	$16.95
Sirloin steak	$18.95

Served w/ fries and soup or salad

BEVERAGES and DESSERTS

Coffee/Tea	$2.50
Soda	$2.00
Ice cream	$3.00
Cake	$4.25

Partner's name	Order
Ex. Ken Adams	Salmon steak, Caesar salad, Coffee, Ice cream

Writing

• ⊙

Choose three items from the menu in **Pair Work** (p. 96) and write them down
on the following receipt. Calculate the tax and subtotal. Decide how much
you want to pay for the tip, and write the total amount of money. Don't
forget to sign your name.

Ex.

Taco beef salad	$ 9.50
Soup of the day	$ 4.50
Cake	$ 4.25
Tax (5%)	$ 0.92
Subtotal	$19.17
Tip	$ 3.83
Total	$23.00

x *Sara Johnson*

Credit Card Receipt

_____	$ _____
_____	$ _____
_____	$ _____
Tax (5%)	$ _____
Subtotal	$ _____
Tip	$ _____
Total	$ _____

x _____

Listening

• ⊙

Part I: Question and Response

Listen to the CD. You will hear a question or statement followed by three
responses. Select the best response to the question or statement.

1. (A) (B) (C)   **2.** (A) (B) (C)

Part II: Short Conversation

Listen to the CD. You will hear a short conversation.
Select the best answer to each question.

1. Who is Joe?

   (A) A client   (B) A server   (C) The owner

2. What did the woman order?

   (A) Lasagna, soup, and garlic toast   (B) Lasagna, salad, and garlic toast

   (C) Lasagna, soup, and salad

Appendix

Unit 2: Letter Styles

Full-block Style

Wahoo Corporation
6-5 Umeda, Kita-ku, Osaka-shi
Osaka 530-0001 Japan — ①

May 14, 2012 — ②

Ms. Sara Johnson
Marketing Director
ABC Computing
325 Central Avenue — ③
New York, NY 10010
USA

Dear Ms. Johnson, — ④

⑤ — Thank you very much for joining us at 2012 CS Trade Fair. We really appreciate your taking time from your busy schedule to be with us. Your discussion was both interesting and informative.

It was a pleasure having you on the show. We wish you continued success and happiness.

Sincerely yours, — ⑥

Scott Robinson — ⑦

Scott Robinson — ⑧
General Manager — ⑨

Enclosure: Catalogue — ⑩

---

① Letterhead (レターヘッド)　⑥ Complimentary Closing (結語)
② Date (日付け)　⑦ Signature (署名)
③ Inside Address (書中宛名)　⑧ Typed Name (差出人)
④ Salutation (頭語)　⑨ Title (肩書き)
⑤ Body (本文)　⑩ Enclosure (同封物)

▧ Block Style

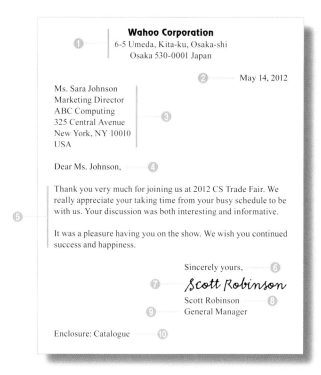

▧ Semi-block Style

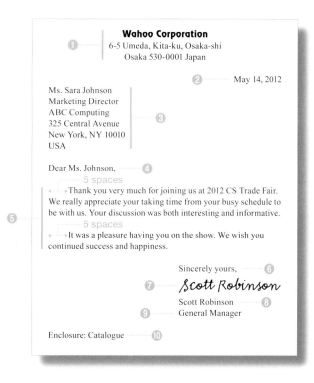

Unit 4: Phonetic Alphabet

A	A as in Adams	**N**	N as in New York
B	B as in Boston	**O**	O as in Ocean
C	C as in Chicago	**P**	P as in Peter
D	D as in Denver	**Q**	Q as in Queen
E	E as in Easy	**R**	R as in Roger
F	F as in Frank	**S**	S as in Sugar
G	G as in George	**T**	T as in Thomas
H	H as in Henry	**U**	U as in Union
I	I as in Italy	**V**	V as in Victor
J	J as in John	**W**	W as in William
K	K as in King	**X**	X as in X-ray
L	L as in London	**Y**	Y as in Young
M	M as in Mary	**Z**	Z as in Zero